The
Way You Look
Tonight

A Play

The Way You Look **Tonight**

A Play

Niall Williams

NEW ISLAND

First published in Ireland in September 2000
by New Island Books
2 Brookside
Dundrum Road
Dublin 14

A CIP catalogue record for this book is available from the
British Library

ISBN 1 902602 31 5

The Arts Council
An Chomhairle Ealaíon

New Island Books receives financial assistance from The Arts Council
(An Chomhairle Ealaíon), Dublin, Ireland.

Typeset by New Island Books
Printed in Ireland by Betaprint
Cover design by Slick Fish Design, Dublin
Cover Image by PCC, Dublin

The Way You Look Tonight was commissioned by Druid
Theatre Company who mounted a production of it in the
Druid Lane Theatre. It was first performed there on the
10th December 1998. The cast were:

Katherine/Kate: Britta Smith
Jim/Jimmy: Patrick Waldron
Ger: Jennifer O'Dea
Francis: George Heslin
Nora: Sonya Kelly

Director: Paddy Cunneen
Designer: Francis O'Connor
Movement Director: Paul Johnson
Lighting Design: Paul Russell
Sound Design: Simon Baker
Production Manager: David Stafford
Stage Manager: Monica Fitzpatrick
Assistant Stage Manager: Nicola Teehan

CHARACTERS

Jim Dooley, sixties, the retiring postmaster.

Katherine Dooley, sixties, his invalid wife.

Francis, their son, late-twenties.

Ger, their oldest daughter, mid-twenties.

Nora, their daughter, aged twenty-three.

Katherine, a woman of sixty, sits alone in an armchair in dim light. She is an invalid, her muscles are locked, her hands sit like claws in her lap. Littered about the floor around her a million sweet wrappers of bright coloured foil. Behind her the disconnected telephone switchboard, the hundred wires that lead off the wall, going everywhere, to nowhere. Two armchairs, a small table of newspapers and a bowl of lemons. Some indication upstage of the old sub-post office front door. To stage right some suggestion of a ruined garden, a leafless whitethorn tree, little cluster of blown sweet wrappers about it. To stage right a swing hanging from above. She sits waiting. Sound off-stage of a man in the kitchen. A noise of pots. Stillness. She sits in reverie looking at the old switchboard. Very slowly and with some difficulty she moves her claw-like right hand in a wavering plugging-in that connects only the air in front of her. Then she speaks, very quietly at first.

Katherine: Caherconn, hello? *(Pause)* Caherconn, hello? *(Pause, then)* Doonbeg, two seven. *(Her hand sways plugging in space. She smiles with memory)* There you are now. Go ahead. Caherconn hello? Just a minute, and I'll try her for you, Breda. *(The hand plugs the connection)* Caherconn, hello? Kilmihil Eight. Putting you through. Go ahead now. There's no answer there, Breda, sorry. No, what? Well I saw them passing down the village earlier. Will I try Mangan's for you? You could catch her there. Hold on so. Caherconn, hello? That number again please. New York, 567-7898. Hang up please and I'll call you back Maureen. Hello this is Katherine here, is Margaret there? Hold on so please. She's there now Breda , putting you through. Not at all. Caherconn hello? Yes. I will Tom, J.J. was looking for him for a cow an hour ago. Hold on, I'll see is he over there.

Katherine sits. Nothing. Then the hand climbs the air and plugs into nothing, for her to say:

Katherine: Francis? Ger? Nora? *(Noise of pots from the kitchen. She stops, a whisper)* ... Hello?

She stops, locked there, at last **Jim** *comes from the kitchen with two boiled eggs on a tray.* **Jim** *is a slight man with a light step, he is still a handsome man. There is something about him that is dashing. Like an old black-and-white photograph though it is fading now. He has a gentle, attentive manner to his wife.*

Jim: Dinner. *(Appearing before **Katherine**)* Here you go.

Katherine: O, eggs.

Jim: Eggs it is. What he said for you to have. Now. *(Puts down the tray across her lap, then crouches down on one knee to open the eggs and feed her. She tries to move but it is apparent she cannot, and only angles her upper body with difficulty)* Now, wasn't I right?

Katherine: What?

Jim: I told you. You fell asleep.

Katherine: I didn't.

Jim: I told you you would. Time it took to boil the egg.

Katherine: I didn't.

Jim: Hardly in the kitchen and I heard you snoring.

Katherine: You're a terrible liar.

Jim: I came in sure. Danced around you. Said would you like one or two. Two fresh eggs in my fists. And what? *(Snores loudly twice)* Two it is.

Katherine: You make everything up.

Jim: I do. Here. *(Lifts spoon of egg to her. It is under-boiled and soft)*

Katherine: Was it only a few minutes? It seemed like a long time.

Jim: *(Looking at the egg)* Ah flip.

Katherine: What?

Jim: Flippin' egg timer, look at that. Is that two-and-a-half minutes?

Katherine: Looks like an egg.

Jim: Very funny.

Katherine: I wish it was a chop.

Jim: That's funny.

Katherine: I love a chop.

Jim: You can't eat chops.

Katherine: With onions.

Jim: Eggs, Doctor Carty says. You can't chew.

Katherine: And mushrooms.

Jim: All right, now.

Katherine: I'm going to pretend it's chops.

She closes her eyes, he cannot move the spoon. He looks at her, almost has to bite his lip from trembling. She opens her eyes.

Katherine: Well?

Jim: We don't eat chops on spoons.

Katherine: God! Give it to me!

He pauses, then waves his fingers over it.

Katherine: What's that?

Jim: Chops and onions. We've no mushrooms.

He brings the spoonful of boiled egg to her lips, and she tastes it.
She eats incredibly slowly. He waits.

Katherine: Mmmm. That's lovely.

Jim: Do you like the way I cooked it?

Katherine: You're a master.

Jim: I am, all right. I'm very proud of my onions.

Katherine: Mmm. You're good to make them for me.

Jim: I am. Only took two-and-a-half minutes. Here.

Katherine: Did you get them at Nolans?

Jim: Nolans?

Katherine: For the Saturday lunch.

Jim *begins to look at his watch; she may be truly confused, he stops himself.*

Jim: Saturday … it's—

Katherine: We're closed one to two, Saturday: chops and onions. Like clockwork. Bring in the *Press* from the counter. Pull the blind, hope the switch won't ring. *(Smiles)* Wouldn't any Christian know it's our dinnertime, love. Lovely, lovely time.

Jim: You're not going mad on me are you?

Katherine: Aren't you mad on me?

Jim: Here, open. *(Feeds her the egg)*

Katherine: What's the news out at the counter?

Jim: Kate, sure we're/

Katherine: *(Eyes closed)* Anybody unusual in this *(Stressing the words)* Saturday morning?

Jim: *(Pause, spooning more egg)* No, Love.

Katherine: *(Moans. Then whispers)* Please.

Jim: Just/

Katherine: Yes?

Jim: The new Mrs McInerney.

Katherine: Was she?

Jim: She was.

Katherine: She must be happy. Married again.

Jim: Danced in like a cow in ballet shoes.

Katherine: And the size of her. Poor woman.

Jim: Not eggs she's on. How'd such a big woman get into such small shoes. You'd swear she'd topple.

Katherine: She's happy anyhow. *(Eats, eyes closed)* It was a lovely morning, wasn't it?

Jim: It rai— … yes, yes, it was.

Katherine: That's what I thought this morning walking down Church Street. I had a skip in my step so I did. Just da-da, a little. And the sunshine! The children were with me. Ger keeps letting go of Nora's hand and running on ahead. She's as wild.

Jim: *(Meaning Katherine)* You'd wonder where she got it. Here, open. *(Feeds her)*

Katherine: *(She feels shell in her mouth)* Agh! What's that? *(Brings it to her tongue)*

Jim: Bit of gristle.

Katherine: Are you trying to poison me?

Jim: You have me now.

Katherine: Wouldn't surprise me. Just waiting for them to shut us today.

Jim: That's right.

Katherine: They close us down, turn off the switch, and now you're a free man.

Jim: Who'd have me if I wasn't?

Katherine: Retired postmaster's a nice catch.

Jim: Probably has a load of old stamps under his mattress.

Katherine: Just poison off the old bag in the chair.

Jim: With a few of Nellie Coughlan's eggs.

Katherine: And ...

Jim: Bingo! Now why didn't I think of that? *(Pause, dabs at her)* You're all stains.

Katherine: I think I'll have chicken tomorrow.

Jim: I'm only rubbing them in.

Katherine: Or turkey. We should have a turkey.

Jim: I think I saw one in the garden. I'll shoot it for you after the tea.

Katherine: They were lovely chops. Thank you.

Jim *rises with a little difficulty, stiffness, taking tray. As he stands the eggcups spill sideways off the tray onto her lap.*

Jim: O flipit!

Katherine: Jim!

Jim: I'm sorry.

Katherine: Are you all right?

Jim says nothing. He reaches into his pocket and takes out a handkerchief. Bends down and cleans the stains and tidies the shells back onto the tray. He has a rage of grief he is trying to contain. Crushes an eggshell.

Katherine: Jim?

He says nothing. He is kneeling cleaning the floor. He has to move one of her legs a fraction to do it.

Jim: *(Getting up again)* Now.

He exits with the tray. **Katherine** *watches him go.*

Katherine: O Jim. *(Calls softly then)* Francis? Ger? Nora?

She waits, turns slightly, gazes at the space of the garden. Suddenly the lights dazzle as through the back come tumbling three figures. They are **Francis**, **Nora** *and* **Ger** *as young children. Helter-skelter, head over heels they tumble forward with giddy cries and shrieks. To the tree.* **Katherine** *watches them.*

Katherine: *(Delighted)* Stop it Francie!

Nora: *(To* **Francis** *as he tumbles into her)* Stop it! Francie!

Francis: Ow!

Ger: You two!

Nora: I was winning.

Francis: You were not.

Ger: *(Standing up, arms wide)* I'm flying away.

Francis: *(Leaping up, aeroplane)* Me too. Neee-aawww!

Nora: *(On the ground)* I'm not.

Francis: I'll fly over you.

Ger: *(Runs about the tree)* I'm going to … India!

Francis: *(Arms out)* Come on Nora, it's no fun.

Nora: I thought we were in the circus.

Ger: *(As she flies by)* It's a flying circus.

Francis: *(Hand to **Nora** who rises)* Flying trapeze! Come on!

Nora: *(As **Francis** pulls her along, running aeroplane)* This isn't how you do trapeze.

Ger: *(Flying by)* It is in our circus.

Francis: *(Flying, calling)* We're magic, aren't we Ger?

Ger: I'm going to crash! I'm going to crash! Help!

Francis: Quick Nora! *(To **Ger**)* Land on us. We'll catch you! Come on.

Nora: Planes can't catch.

Francis: O Nora.

Ger: Aaaahhhhh!

Francis: Quick. Down our wings. Like this.

Ger falls down on top of them, fit of giggles as all three tumble on the ground. They lie there together a moment.

Francis: We made it.

Nora: How did we do it? How did we catch her?

Francis: Magic, wasn't it Ger?

Ger: You nearly didn't.

Nora: But I don't understand. How can/

Francis: You can't understand it. Nobody can. That's what's so brilliant. Absolutely brilliant.

Ger: I love the smell here.

Nora: Where?

Ger: Here. In the garden. This time of year, when the leaves are down. *(She breathes an armful of the sweet wrappers)*

Francis: *(Breathing them)* It's sweet.

Ger throws them up so they fall into their lying down faces.

Nora: *(One hand throwing them upwards)* Imagine they're sweets. Mmmmmm.

Francis: Here. Lets make a clock.

Ger: A clock?

Nora: Why?

Francis: Because then we can move it. It can be tea time.

Ger: Yes.

They lie on the ground amidst the leaves, and make the shape of a clock.

Francis: Who's the hands?

Ger: I am.

Nora: I want to be. I never get to and I'm the youngest.

Ger: All right. Nora's the hands. And I'm the hands and Francis is. It's our special clock. The Dooley clock.

Francis: With three times.

Ger: All the time. Yes.

Francis: Brilliant.

Ger: All right. It's five o'clock. *(Makes it with her feet and hands)*

Francis: And six o'clock.

Nora: And seven o'clock.

Ger: Teatime!

Francis: Teatime teatime!

Jim: *(Entering with a mug of tea and tablets)* Teatime.

The children lie there. **Katherine** *gazes at them.*

Jim: You're not snoring? *(No reply a moment)* Kate, love?

Katherine: *(Turning to him)* Thank you.

Jim holds the mug for her to drink, his hand and hers on it as she takes a slow sip, pause for her to swallow.

Jim: That's tea, you know?

Katherine: *(Smiles)* Very nice.

Jim: Good. More?

Katherine: *(Drinks again, their hands on the cup; it seems to take forever for her just to take a drink. She swallows, nods. He crouches beside her, waiting for each sip)* Do you know what I'm thinking?

Jim: Of course I do.

Katherine: Of the children. I think about them all the time.

Jim: I suppose there's no harm in it.

Katherine: Of where they are, of what they could be doing. Right now.

Jim: Do you make the time changes?

Katherine: What?

Jim: Except for Leitrim. Leitrim's on our time, far as we know.

Katherine: I can't even have a conversation with you.

Jim: *(Gives her more tea)* That's why I'm poisoning you. Here.

Pause, she drinks, looks to the garden.

Katherine: We planted everything in the wrong place, in the garden.

Jim: We should have planted in the kitchen?

Katherine: *(Sips)* It's the way things grow. You never think of it. How they all tangle up later on. It's the thorny things that take over.

Jim: Of course it is. Now. O flipit. *(Looks at tablet for her)* Pink one. Blue ones in the evening. You've had your pink one.

He pushes on the arm of the chair to get up. Pauses. Pushes himself up again. Stands, wavers.

Katherine: You'd miss the calls, wouldn't you?

Jim stops, then walks on.

Katherine: Even times when they were a nuisance.

Jim: *(Exiting into kitchen)* Which was often.

Katherine: They'd be there, anyhow. There'd always be someone, voices on the other end. *(Pause)*

Francis and Nora sit up, back to back, as adults.

Francis: Nora, it's Francis.

Nora: *(Sleepy)* Hello. God Francis, what time is it? What time is it there?

Francis: I'm sorry. I didn't mean to wake you.

Nora: I don't know what time it is in California Francis, but it's three o'clock in the morning here.

Francis: I know. I'm sorry.

Nora: Are you all right?

Francis: Yes. It's just ...

Nora: God!

Francis: What?

Nora: Nothing. Go on.

Francis: If this is a bad time?

Nora: No, it's wonderful. It's absolutely great. Francis it's three o'clock.

Francis: I'll call back.

Nora: Is this about Mam?

Francis: I'll call tomorrow.

Nora: Francis? No, Francis?

Francis walks away.

Nora: Shite.

Nora walks away. Ger sits up, walks to the swing, then looks directly over at her mother.

Ger: *(Very softly)* Do you know what I'm thinking right now? Do you? Can you? I'm so far away from you. I'm a

nurse here in Africa. And you're there. You're sitting there.
You're just sitting there all the time, aren't you? *(The grief of
it hits her. She pauses)* And if you were here. *(Long pause)*
That's a game I play sometimes. When I miss you. When I
want to show you things here. *(Gets onto the swing, stands,
swings)* The desert. The way the sun changes everything
about the way you feel every day. *(Pause)* I sent you the
lemons I picked in Algeria the morning I woke up with the
smell of them in the room. I wished you could have walked
out under the trees with me that morning. The smell of
them, going out and just reaching up and picking them, it
was so … so not like home. I think that's what I love about
it here, the freedom. The sun on your body all the time
makes it feel like it's … broken free, like you can feel the life
of every inch of you and not be wrapped up in some winter
coat in the rain. It's like the world is a different place here
and the things you grew up thinking are not so true
anymore. *(She closes her eyes to the sunlight, swings)* O Mam.

Katherine *makes a small groan.* **Jim** *appears with the tablets.*
Ger *walks off.*

Jim: Did you say something?

Katherine: No.

Jim: I thought you said something.

Katherine: Good job you're not on the switch so.

Jim: What do you mean?

Katherine: What you were famous for. Hearing things.
Why'd you think they called you 'Ears'?

Jim: I know nothing. About anything that goes on here. I'm
a simple civil servant.

Katherine: Retired.

Jim: Since five o'clock.

Katherine: Did they say something about a museum?

Jim: They want to set it up in a museum. Last operating switchboard in Ireland. Maybe they might set you sitting up alongside it if you want? Museum pieces.

Katherine: It could be nice.

Jim: O yes.

Katherine: I belong in a museum.

Jim: You do all right.

Katherine: My chin.

Jim: That much anyway.

Katherine: The Hassett chin, belongs in a museum.

Jim: What about the mouth with it? *(**Katherine** laughs)* Here. *(**Jim** gives her the tablet. She has difficulty swallowing it, finally succeeds)* I'm going to sit down now, all right?

*Pause. **Jim** sits. Lifts a newspaper.*

Katherine: You're free of it now.

Jim: What?

Katherine: The switch. We couldn't really manage it anymore anyway.

Jim: Of course we could.

Katherine: You didn't want them to take it out today. It's my fault.

Jim: *(Puts down newspaper)* Kate.

Katherine: I take up all your time.

Jim: Don't Kate. *(Pause)* I'm trying to read the paper.

Katherine: Yes.

Jim: Do you want anything?

Katherine: No.

Jim: Will I bring you into the room?

Katherine: I'm all right. I want to wait here for Francis.

Jim: Francis? Nora you mean.

Katherine: Did I say Francis?

Jim: Nora. Sure she won't be down until tomorrow. She won't finish teaching before four o'clock, home to feed the children, something for Paddy coming in. Dark, and that road from Leitrim. Tomorrow she'll be here.

Katherine: She said she might be down this evening. How do I look? Do I look all right?

Jim: You look fine.

*Pause. **Jim** begins to read his newspaper.*

Katherine: Jim, I need to go to the bathroom.

Jim: You just went before you dozed off.

Katherine: I need to go.

Jim: You don't.

Katherine: I do.

Jim: Are you sure? *(**Katherine** doesn t answer)* All right, right then.

***Francis** enters beneath tree.*

Francis: Right then.

Jim shuffles and brings out a wheelchair, he parks it alongside her chair. Following plays as he goes to pick her up under the arms. The kids scene following is in fact overlapping at first.

Katherine: Careful Jim.

Jim: *(Struggling)* This is careful! Come on now, let your weight, that's it, get it, will you try and let yourself, come on, *(Gets her into the chair crookedly)* wait now, wait. *(Goes behind her to pull her into upright sitting position)* There, now. *(Pauses for breath)* Now. *(Sighs, blows)* Either you're getting heavy or I'm getting weak. Better cut back on the eggs.

Katherine: It's the sweets.

Jim: God no, couldn't be. Must be the chops.

Katherine: Go on.

Jim: What?

Katherine: Making me fat. Say it.

Jim: Heavy.

Katherine: And fat.

Jim: Come on.

Jim gets her into the wheelchair, breathes, wheels her off towards the bathroom. The wheelchair has a dodgy wheel, and so the journey is wavering, zigzag.

Katherine: There! Over there, that's the bathroom.

Jim: *(Panting)* Is that right?

Katherine: You're going to miss it.

Jim: Poison's affecting your brain.

*He struggles but just as he is about to reverse her in, **Katherine** rises. **Jim** wheels the chair in as if she is still in.*

Jim: Here now, we're here. *(Exits)*

Ger *runs on. She looks about the emptiness. Then* **Francis** *and* **Nora** *come running after her.* **Katherine** *stands and watches them in delight.*

Ger: We're here!

Francis: *(To **Ger**)* You're too fast!

Ger: I am not!

Nora: *(Annoyed)* You are so. You wouldn't wait for us.

Ger: Amn't I waiting now? Even though we're going to be late.

Francis: We won't be.

Nora: She just wanted to go in without us. She wanted to see Tommy Eyres!

Ger: Shutup! I did not!

Nora: Did too. Tommy Tommy Tommy!

Francis: Stoppit Nora. Stop. Ger's going to come with us. We're all going to stay together, aren't we Ger?

Ger: I don't care about Tommy Eyres.

Francis: That's what Mam and Dad said. We could all go if/

Ger: Tommy Eyres may be there and he may not be there, and I may say hello to him if I feel like it, and I may not. Doesn't mean a thing.

Nora: God I hear them!

Francis: What? Come on!

They rush down the street to the Community Hall.

Katherine: We're too late.

Nora: We're too late!

Francis: No we're not.

Nora: We're late.

Ger: We're not. That's just records.

Katherine: They never start on time.

Ger: They never start on time.

They form an excited queue.

Francis: Don't push. I have the money.

Ger: We don't need money.

Francis: Mammy gave it to me.

Ger: Keep it for sweets. It'll be Johnny Hehir on the door. He won't take anything from us.

Nora: I want a mineral.

Francis: But/

Ger: We should be in for free.

Francis: I don't want to go in for free.

Ger: Don't be stupid Francie. Come on.

Nora: I bet they win.

Ger: I bet they do too.

Nora: They're the best.

Francis: The McInerney Family Singers are good.

Ger: *(Disbelief)* God!

Francis: Daddy says so.

Ger: They're rubbish.

Francis: How do you know?

Ger: *(Rock-sings)* The Gypsy Rover came over the hill, ya-dee-do-ya-dee day-ooo! *(**Katherine** laughs)*

Nora: They're not as good as us.

Ger: No way.

Ger and **Katherine**: We're the best.

Nora: *(Looks forward, calls to interrupt them)* Ger we're next! Come on!

Ger takes the front.

Ger: Let me, come on. I'll ask him.

The 'Gypsy Rover music comes on loud.

Ger: Look at them, they're nothing. They're not like us. We're …

Nora: Full of moon.

Ger And grace and light and satin dresses.

Francis: And shiny blue shoes …

*They move in a semi-circle to a position where they peer forward toward the imaginary stage. Song ends. Then the opening music of 'The Continental begins. The lights pop up and **Katherine** as **Kate** steps up to join **Jim** as **Jimmy** coming out dancing à la Astaire and Rogers. They are wonderful and light together, dancing their routine in the Community Hall Talent Show. Their children watch delightedly, laughing and happy as **Jimmy** turns **Kate** across the floor. They dance. It is a moment of pure romance and magic. As the songs ends the children burst into applause,*

Jimmy and Kate take their bows and exit stage left leaving the children to spin, dancing and humming the tune, into the garden. They all three dance a wild continental about the tree and then melt down among the leaves as, a moment later, Jimmy and Kate come in the post office door in the early hours after the show. They carry the trophy.

Kate: *(Standing removing her shoes)* Shush!

Jimmy: *(Removing his shoes)* I am shush.

Kate: Shush!

Jimmy: *(Mimes/Mounts the words)* All ... right. Are-they-asleep?

Kate: *(Raises a finger, steps towards where the children are lying, then whispers)* They're in dreamland.

Jimmy: Just like us. *(Taking her into dance rhythm, both holding their shoes)* Lada-dedah, lada-dedah. We were magnificent.

Kate: *(Dancing)* We?

Jimmy: The Dancing Dooleys. Jimmy and Kate.

Kate: We?

Jimmy: You. You, you you you.

Kate: Thank you. *(Dances the shoes up to him)* You were passable yourself Fred.

Jimmy: *(Reaches in his pocket, gives her a wrapped chocolate)* The lengths I go to.

Kate: *(Taking the sweet)* That's nothing compared to my usual lovers.

Jimmy: Is that right?

Kate: Gospel. There was a fellow once.

Jimmy: There was?

Kate: Was in a certain line of work.

Jimmy: Night work.

Kate: Exactly.

Jimmy: And day work.

Kate: More or less. I was only a girl.

Jimmy: Slip of a thing.

Kate: Kate-Hassett — that — was my name.

Jimmy: You were a mouthful.

Kate: I'll relieve you now, I says, when I came across the street and took the nightshift from him.

Jimmy: O painful. *(Rises and stands close behind her)* Your lover?

Kate: That one, yes.

Jimmy: And what did he say?

Kate: He says, 'Would you like a sucker Kate?'.

Jimmy: The devil romantic.

Kate: Great line he had. I only eat chocolates I told him.

Jimmy: Right too. The sweetness of you.

Kate: Do you know what he did?

Jimmy: Can't imagine.

Kate: The very next night I came across for the shift/

Jimmy: /he had his pockets stuffed with chocolates, a hundred of them, emptied out of a big box into the bulging pockets of his jacket. Ruined the line of it.

Kate: For all he cared.

Jimmy: Poor man stayed on with you and it not even his own shift.

Kate: He did.

Jimmy: *(Hands going around her, fingers holding a chocolate in each)* Must have been awful?

Kate: *(She takes a sweet, drops wrapper)* He was good for chocolates anyway.

Kate laughs and Jimmy kisses her.

Jimmy: He was a young fella?

Kate: O God he was.

Jimmy: Handsome?

Kate: Passable enough.

Jimmy: I heard he was the dashingest man in Clare.

Kate: *(Laughs)* Where'd you hear that old lie?

Jimmy: Women were only mad after him.

Kate: Is that what you heard? Tell me.

Jimmy: He could go out on an evening from the post office in his dark suit and his shoes spit-clean, stars shining off them all the way back to Kilkee, walking like he was dancing.

Kate: Between the cow dungs.

Jimmy: Not a hair out of place.

Kate: With gobs of Brylcream.

Jimmy: And when he got to the Atlantic Ballroom the ladies'd be only swooning to dance with him.

Kate: Must have been the shoes.

Jimmy: Shoes what. Man was like a spinning top. Something out of circus he was.

Kate: A clown?

Jimmy: A dancing man. They never saw a foxtrotter like him back there.

Kate: The hound.

Jimmy: *(Produces another chocolate, offers it)* So, was that the one?

Kate: *(Nods)* My lover.

Jimmy: God but weren't you the lucky lady.

Kate: Sure you have to settle for something.

Jimmy and Kate laugh. He kisses her and pulls her to her feet, and they sway a few dance-steps. As they do, Ger gets onto the swing. Nora sits. They look in opposite directions. Then, as Jimmy exits and Katherine stands at the bathroom door, the sisters are on the phone to each other, twenty-five years later. They speak, connected but invisible to each other. Francis climbs and sits in the tree.

Ger: *(Excited)* Nora?

Nora: Ger? I can hardly hear you. Can you hear me?

Ger: Yes, yes. How are you?

Nora: Where are you?

Ger: I'm in Niarobi, Nora.

Nora: Yes?

Ger: *(Shouts)* I'm in love!

Nora: *(Quiet)* Again?

Ger: O God Nora it's wonderful. I met him at the hospital. He's/

Nora: Where's he from?

Ger: Algeria.

Nora: Algeria? Ger, he's from Algeria? Is he …/

Ger: I know you liked Peter, but/

Nora: I thought it was Mark?

Ger: God, that was ages ago, that was nothing, forget him.

Nora: *(Under her breath)* And Peter/

Ger: It's … O Nora I can't describe it. He's just wonderful. I had the week off, and we went to Kilamanjaro. Can you believe it? I can't. Nora, it's like I just found out what life is.

Nora: *(Sceptical)* O yes?

Ger: Like I was shot off a rocket, like I'd never seen anything before and now everything is just … just like it's got a thin sheen on it. Like everything's shining. You know? O God, Nora. You know what? I love just … just touching him/

Nora *(Under her breath)* /Shite.

Ger: /His skin's like I don't what it's like. Like you want to just eat it/

Nora: *(Sarcastic)* Lovely.

Ger: What?

Nora: Nothing Ger.

Pause.

Ger: Well, I had to talk to somebody. I wanted to ... I'm so happy Nora I'm terrified.

Nora: You don't sound it.

Ger: It's, you know, this. This feeling, like dancing together or something, you know, in the air and ... O I can't describe it.

Nora: No.

Ger: Have you heard from Francie? I tried him but I couldn't get anyone. What time is it in California?

Nora: He's probably sleeping. He only calls me when I'm asleep.

Ger: I want to wake him up. I want to talk to him. This is what Francie needs, to fall in love, to be head over heels Nora.

Nora: She'd have to have some unstable particles, subatomic something or other to interest our professor.

Ger: I know. He's lost in it, isn't he?

Nora: *(Imitating **Francis**)* You're never lost in physics, you just don't understand what it is you've discovered.

Ger: You know Nora, right now, this is the best time in my life. Everything seems so great it's like it's too good, that it can't be true, like I'm going to wake up and it's going to be over and the feeling will be gone and none of it will have been real. You know?

Nora: O yeah. *(Pause)* Well Francis is the one to talk to then.

Ger: Why?

Nora: Well he's our expert on reality. He's the one able to explain things I never heard of and you never heard of and nobody seems too sure even exist. So I'm sure he could help you all right. *(Pause, realises her anger)* Sorry. He's from Algeria, Ger?

Ger: Hadji/

Nora: *(Lines fades)* What? Where? I can't hear you. Ger?

Ger: I'm running out of money. *(Louder)* How's Mam and Dad?

Nora: Mam is … *(**Jim** is now out of bathroom with wheelchair and **Katherine** has slipped back into it and they are making their way back to the armchair as **Nora** stares at them)* … fine. Fine Ger.

Ger: And Patrick and the boys?

Nora: O we're …

Ger: *(Shouts)* I've got to go Nora.

Nora: … wonderful.

Ger: I'll call again. Tell everyone …

Silence falls between them.

Nora: *(Softly)* Yes.

*They rise and go off in opposite directions, leaving **Francis** there in the tree.*

Jim: Now.

Katherine: What time is it, Jim?

Jim: Do you want to see a programme?

Katherine: Is it raining? I hope Nora is not hurrying in the rain.

Jim: She's not hurrying. She mightn't even be coming tonight.

Katherine: She knows the switch was being turned off today. She said she'd be down.

Jim: We should have a retirement party. La-de-dah, de de dah dah.

Jim hums and wheels the chair very slightly as if in dance with it.

Katherine: Jim?

Jim: Yes?

Katherine: *(Bites her lip)* Nothing.

Jim: What is it?

Katherine: I don't want to ask you. *(Turns from her reflection)* I just look so ... I'm ... I'm so ...

Jim: *(Tenderly)* What is it? What's the matter? Stop. Stop now. What do you want? Tell me. Don't be crying. Don't. Do you want me to get something?

Katherine: I look ...

Jim: Shush. I'll get your bag.

Katherine: *(Softly)* My blue cardigan.

Jim: What?

Katherine: My blue cardigan.

Jim: Yes, blue cardigan all right.

*He exits. She sits facing front as **Francis** sits up and looks down toward her.*

Francis: *(Five years old)* Mammy.

Katherine: Francie pet.

Francis: I can't sleep mammy. Tell me a story.

Katherine: I already told you three. Amn't I telling you stories all the night?

Francis: Tell me one more, Mammy. Just one more. And that's all. Promise.

Katherine: And what'll you do if you can't sleep then?

Francis: I will. I'll be fast asleep with the story. I can sleep with stories better. Tell me one like the one about Africa, or the flying family, that's a good one, yes that's a good one, where we're all flying.

Katherine: It's dancing really.

Francis: Dancing and flying.

Katherine: Through the air.

Francis: Yes.

Katherine: The little boy and his two sisters and their Mammy and Daddy can't get to sleep one night. None of them can, and they all go in and out of each others' rooms.

Francis: In and out.

Katherine: To see is the other one asleep. Because there's a big moon that night, big and silky, and it's shining in everywhere. It's in the landing window and all along the floor upstairs like a silvery carpet and the more they walk on it the more they notice that they aren't feeling it underneath their feet anymore.

Francis: The little boy.

Katherine: The little boy notices it first. He notices his feet aren't touching the floor at all. He takes little bouncy steps and he springs along with his mammy and his daddy and his two sisters behind. 'Hey, look at me, I'm dancing,' he says. And the next thing you know, they're all dancing, the whole family, dancing along together across the moony carpet. They dance right to the edge of the window where the moonlight is shining in. And then, pop!

Francis: *(Giggles)* Pop!

Katherine: Out the window dances the little boy!

Francis: Pop!

Katherine: Out dances his sister.

Francis: Pop!

Katherine: Out dances his other sister. Right out along the moonlight dancing.

Francis: And flying!

Katherine: Yes

Francis: 'Cause they're magic.

Katherine: They are. And the mammy and daddy watch from the window as the children dance and fly about in the moonlight outside the house.

Francis: Aaw. I want the daddy and mammy to come out.

Katherine: No, they watch. They aren't so magic as the others. But they have to keep watching. And it's a lovely time.

Francis: And it goes on a long time?

Katherine: It does. Until the moonlight is all danced up and gets thinner and thinner, and the children's legs dance slower and slower and slower and slower, and they get sleepier and sleepier.

Francis sleeps, as *Jim* returns with the blue cardigan.

Jim: Now. This is the one.

Katherine: Thank you.

Jim takes off the bib and the blue cardigan she is wearing with some difficulty. She cannot move and he moves her to free the cardigan, incurring great effort. As he lets it fall to the floor, it gets caught in the wheelchair. He pulls at it. Manages to get it on her and button it. It should be apparent how even this simple thing has been a difficult physical dance of two near-broken bodies.

Jim: That's nice now. *(Pointing at the make-up bag)* Do you want this? Kate?

Katherine: *(Nods slowly, whispers)* Please.

Jim: *(Unsure)* Yes?

Katherine: Thank you.

Jim opens the bag and takes out her hairbrush. He pauses a moment before her and then very softly brushes her hair. After a bit ...

Jim: You should have asked me to have Mary over to do you. She would have come.

Katherine: Over.

Jim: Come over, yes.

Katherine: Over.

Jim: What?

Katherine: *(To the mirror)* The hair, there, brush it over, there.

Jim: This?

Katherine: *(Tries to show him with wavering hand)* Brush it there.

Jim: *(He does with uncertainty)* She'd come over anytime to do your face, your hair. Just because we don't need her for the switch anymore doesn't mean.

Katherine: *(Sharply)* No!

Jim: She's very accommodating. You should use her more often. Do you know?

Katherine: I like you to do it.

Jim: *(Finishes)* Now. Lovely.

Katherine: As an old potato.

Jim: Stop that.

Katherine: *(Sing-song)* Somebody smells like pee.

Jim: Ah Kate.

Katherine: It-must-be-me! *(Indicating the make-up bag)* Will you put a little something on me?

Jim: You're grand.

Katherine: Please.

*Pause. **Jim** opens the make-up bag.*

Katherine: Perfume.

Jim: This?

Katherine: Abracadabra.

She nods, he tips some on his finger, pauses a moment at where to put it, then as she moves her head to the side he dabs her neck. She turns her head to the other side and he repeats it.

Jim: Now.

Katherine: More.

Jim: You're fine Kate.

Katherine: Somebody smells like …

Jim: All right …

He tips the bottle into the palm of his hand and splashes it out, then applies it to her wrists, her hands.

Jim: Happy?

Katherine: Will you put some on my legs?

Jim: On your legs?

Katherine: So I can be dancing.

Jim: I'm nearly dancing myself with the whiff of you.

Katherine: *(Wry smile)* I like to have an effect.

Jim: Right, right, righto. *(He pours perfume into his hand and then dabs some on her calves)*

Katherine: I like it when you touch my legs. It makes me feel they're still there. *(He cannot look at her)* Am I beautiful?

Jim: *(Putting away the perfume)* You are.

Katherine: *(Half-laugh)* What a liar I married. *(Uncomfortable moment)* I need a bit more.

Jim: Any more and you'd pass out.

Katherine: My face, Jim.

A moment.

Jim: I would have got Mary Mulvihill. You should have said …

Katherine: Please.

Jim: *(Opening the powder, he begins to dab her face. Continues through the following)* We did this this morning for the Telecom people coming.

*The three children appear together, peering in at the mother and father. **Nora** has her 'blankey .*

Katherine: *(Closes her eyes a moment, then slowly)* We're on tonight.

Jim: What?

Katherine: We're on stage in half an hour.

Jim: Kate maybe you/

Katherine: *(Gently)* Shush.

*As **Jim** applies her make-up, the children are watching. Then **Ger** squats and **Nora** behind her combs her hair, and **Francis** behind **Nora** combs hers, all facing the parents.*

Katherine: *(Speaking slowly)* We're going to be dancing. We have everything laid out in the room upstairs. My dress, my shoes. They're the silver ones Francis says are like I've stepped in moonlight. My hair, my long long hair is combed out and pinned up. *(Hums)* Da-de-da dahdah, da-de-de-dah-dah. *(Pouts)* I'm putting on my face.

Jim: *(Whispers)* You're putting on your neck if you don't keep still.

Katherine: We're covered on the switch. Say her name.

Jim: Mary?

Katherine: Mary Mulvihill, she's here and your black shoes are up and down the stairs to me, Clickclack, clickclack. Are you ready yet? It takes more than a few minutes for a lady to be as beautiful as I have to be.

Jim: To be dancing with me is it?

Katherine: O yes. As if you didn't think you were Fred Astaire himself.

Jim: Me? I'm just a dancing man. They call me 'Ears'.

Katherine: They call you more than that.

Jim: What?

Katherine: Nothing. Lips. *(Pouts her lips. He rustles in the bag for the lipstick)*

Jim: You don't have any.

Katherine: Lips?

Jim: I can't find … here.

*It is an old lipstick and a garish shade. When **Jim** opens it the tip of it falls out of the holder onto the floor. He retrieves it, tries to push it back into the holder. He cleans it on the inside of his hand, then begins to put it on her.*

Jim: Keep still.

Katherine: What's our first number?

Jim: God, that perfume's very strong.

Katherine: 'Night and Day'.

Jim: Yes. *(His hand shakes badly. He paints it above her upper lip)* Flipit!

Katherine: *(Eyes closed, whispering)* 'Night and Day, you are the one, day and night, night and day.'

Jim: Kate! Stop it. I can't … *(Kate stops)* Feck. *(He picks out a handkerchief, touches it to his mouth and then rubs her lip clean like a child s)*

Katherine: Ow! That hurts.

Jim: Sorry. The bloody thing isn't going on right. *(Tries again to apply it evenly. Hand shakes, smudges)* Feck. Shite!

Katherine: *(Opens her eyes)* Jim.

Jim: I'm sorry, I — *(Smudges it again)* Damnit!

He throws the lipstick away. Then steps away from her leaving her with smudged mouth. He is upset and moves away to regain himself.

Katherine: Jim. Don't. It doesn't matter. Please Jim, wait.

*But he is walking away, more upset than he should be, then he is gone into kitchen. **Katherine** groans.*

Katherine: Ooooh! *(Then, very softly, to no one)* I just like it. I like you to be touching me.

*From the kitchen, we hear whisky being poured from bottle. **Katherine** looks to where the children are. **Ger** stands up, pulls up **Francis**.*

Ger: *(To **Francis**)* I'm in love with you.

Nora: That's not fair.

Ger: He's my husband.

Nora: *(Getting up, linking him)* No he's mine. Aren't you Francis?

Ger: We got married.

Nora: So did we.

Ger: You were the bridesmaid silly, remember?

Nora: That's not fair. That wasn't today.

Ger: Doesn't matter. We're still married. Aren't we Jimmy?

Francis: I'm married to both of you.

Nora: You can't be.

Ger: Yes he can.

Nora: How?

Francis: I'm magic. I can be in two places at one time.

Nora: Really?

Francis: Yep.

Ger: Brilliant.

Francis: First I'm here with Kate. Right?

Ger: *(Links **Francis**)* And we're going to a dance.

Nora: I don't like dances.

Ger: You're not coming. You're minding the switch.

Francis: You're Mary.

Ger: You're Mary.

Nora: I don't like her.

Francis: Okay, you're/

Nora: Helen Igoe/

Ger: How can you be Helen Igoe, she's your teacher.

Nora: You said it was magic.

Francis: All right. That's who you are.

Ger: *(Grabbing Francis)* And you're here with me.

Nora: *(Taking his arm)* And me.

Ger: *(Moves with him)* Now we have to go to our dance.

Nora: *(Moves opposite direction)* And we have to be at home.

Francis: Aghh! Wait! Stop now. *(To **Ger**)* You are at your dance. Go on, dance!

Ger: But I want to dance with you.

Francis: I am with you. Close your eyes. Go on, dance.

Ger *starts dancing with invisible partner.*

Francis: *(To **Nora**)* And we're sitting down at home. *(He sits her down on the floor)* Reading books.

Nora: We're playing our fiddles. Mrs Igoe plays her fiddle.

Francis: All right. Our fiddles.

Nora *mimes fiddle-playing. The music begins to come up.*
Francis *is standing miming fiddle with **Nora** as **Ger** is dancing.*
*He sways, then he is dancing and fiddling. He is flying across the room and back, is in the two places at once, fiddling with **Nora**, and then dancing with **Ger**, in the two lives, the two loves, until*
Katherine *calls out and the scene instantly dissolves.*

Katherine: Francis! Francis! *(Cries out)* Agh! Stopit stopit!

*They are gone. **Katherine** makes a little groaning sound, then another slightly higher. She tries to clear her throat of something. Through the following her mouth will begin to feel thick with a strange tongue. She speaks first out of memory: to make the children present and to cure herself. But she arrives at the place where her illness keeps breaking in on her. She begins with eyes closed.*

Katherine: My dress and my things are ... laid out. Laid out on the bed. I am putting on my face. My Jimmy, my

Jimmy keeps coming and going up and down the stairs
from Mary at the switch. Clickclack, clickclack, Are you
ready yet?, landing light shining stars off his shoes.
Clickclack, clickclack. Night and day you are the one. My
dazzling man. Dashingest man in Clare. Am I beautiful
yes? Now. Don't. Don't cry Francis. I have to. You know
Mammy and Daddy have to go out and enjoy themselves
sometime ... I know that. I know that you don't like her,
but she'll be downstairs. You three can stay up here,
pretend it's your own little world, with nothing to disturb it.
You can bring up some biscuits and some milk, and won't
the three of you be like a king and his, his two queens. *(Wry
smile)*

As the adults **Ger** *and* **Francis** *and* **Nora** *now walk out to their
separate corners of the stage, looking away from her.* **Katherine**
*vaguely lifts her arm in giving gestures during the following. They
do not interact with her, they stand apart,* **Ger** *in Africa,* **Nora** *in
Leitrim and* **Francis** *in California.*

Katherine: Now. *(Her voice begins to struggle)* Mammy is
going to give each of you a special little bit of her for you to
take to bed and mind while she's out. Here Nora, take this
for you. This is for Ger, and, let me see, yes, for Francis, my
clever boy. Now, I'm going to take a little bit of all of you
with me too. See. All right? Now, we'll all have some of
each other all the same. And nobody can take it away ...
Like we're all ... co ... co ... *(She is stuck on the word, it takes
an effort to say it at last)* connected. *(No reply, she slumps back,
small cry)* O God.

Ger: The first thing to go will be the vowel sounds. That's
because of the collapse of the diaphragm and the
contraction of the intercostal muscles supporting the
ribcage. Then the consonants become slurred due to the
faulty timing of the impulses to the nerves supplying the
lips, the palate and tongue. *(Pause)* O Mam.

Katherine: No no no no no! *(Pause)* You're going into the silence. Aren't you? It's true, like the doctors said. One plug after the other. *(Very carefully)* Disconnected. You're not going to be able to speak, are you? Caherconn, hello.

Francis, now in the tree, speaks to Nora. Ger sits in the swing.

Francis: Nora it's me.

Nora: Francis, God. I just got in.

Francis: I'm sorry for calling last night. It's ...

Nora: You didn't invent the clock yet, over there? Paddy says to me you must be some professor not to be able to figure out the change in time.

Francis: I'm sorry.

Nora: Unless it's an absolute emergency Francis, I can't. I just can't. That's the way I am. Even if Paddy, he gets the kids in the night if anything. That's just the way it is. I have a screaming class of twenty-five kids to face into, I need my sleep. That's all there is about it.

Francis: Well/

Nora: What?

Francis: You know, how are things?

Nora: Things? What things Francis? The weather's terrible.

Francis: Nora!

Nora: Well why do you never say it? God Francis, why don't you say, this is my monthly phone call to find out how Mam is? Don't you think you could get to that? They have therapists over there don't they?

Francis: What?

Nora: In California. Don't you think you could get one of them to help you see your way through to calling Mother more than 'things'? I mean that can't be very good, can it? 'Things'. How are you Things? Dear Things, lovely to see you. *(Pause, no reply, sighs, takes off one of her shoes and itches her foot)* I'm sorry Francis. I'm tired. I just got in and I've got a husband and two children due in four minutes. Have you any formula for speed-cooking fish fingers?

Francis: Nora I'll call back.

Nora: No, Don't. You might catch me in one of my bad moods … God. she's … She's fine/

Francis: It doesn't sound like it. Are you going down?

Nora: *(Drearily)* Yes. Tomorrow.

Francis: They got switched off today, didn't they?

Nora: Far as I know. They were expecting them to come this morning.

Francis: It feels wrong somehow.

Nora: How can it feel wrong? We're not in the Dark Ages over here any more, you know. We're automatic now. We're Touch-Tone.

Francis: It's just. For them. What'll/

Nora: They'll manage. Like we all do. With reality Francis.

Francis: You think I should come home.

Pause.

Francis: You do, don't you?

Nora: O God, don't Francis. Don't. I haven't the strength for it right now.

Francis: I'm just saying/

Nora: I know, and you want me to say, No Francis, no everything's fine. I have it all under control, go on, stay on there and solve the problems of quantum leaping molecules falling into black holes or whatever the hell it is you do. *(Pause)* Sorry. Listen. Do what you have to. I'm the one in Leitrim. So I have to go down. That's what I have to do. What Ger thinks she has to do is nurse the sick in Africa, avoid getting pregnant or married at all costs and still manage to fall in love with every Tom, Dick and Hadji that passes her way. Calling her sister to tell her this one is 'wonderful' and didn't they just have a fabulous weekend in Killymanjaro or Timbucktoo or somewhere, telling me this while I'm hugging a hot water bottle, mind, with two yelling children fighting over the last sausage. So, what you have to do Francis I don't know. Boring old, wise old younger sister Nora doesn't know. She doesn't even know how the trick of the clocks worked and how she became the oldest one being born the youngest. So you can't ask me. It's not fair. All right? Do your physics, stay in California, carry your mother around everywhere and yet never ever ever speak to your father. That's about it as I see it. That's what you have to do. *(Pause. She realises she has blown and regrets it. She sighs, softly then)* O God, Francie. *(A beat)* Francie? *(He is no longer on the line, she calls)* Francis, *Francis*!

Jim comes out to **Katherine.**

Jim: You were calling.

Katherine: No.

Jim: I thought I heard you calling.

Katherine: He's not coming.

Jim: Nora's coming, Kate, Nora. But it'll be tomorrow now. I told you.

Pause.

Katherine: I'm a mess, amn't I?

Jim: It's my fault. I'll try again.

Katherine: You've had a drink.

Jim: Don't.

Katherine: You walk out and leave me here and have a drink when you're upset with me.

Jim: I'm not upset with you.

Katherine *pauses, about to answer, but doesn't.*

Jim: You look fine. Honestly. *(Produces a sweet for her and unwraps it)* Here, this'll quieten you down. *(Puts it in her mouth, smells powerful perfume)* Whew! *(She looks at him)* Magnificent. Queen of Persia.

Katherine: More lies.

Jim: It's not.

Katherine: I want more. More lies!

Jim: *(Stuck a moment)* O. Em, the moon is out, everybody's happy in the kingdom, the stars, the stars are turned golden, the the/

Katherine: Magic carpet/

Jim: *(Begins to wheel her towards her chair)* The magic carpet is fixed, parked outside, ready for road, *(Catches himself)* I mean sky, the sky-road, and the forecast is good, no more rain, ever, which is handy for magic carpets, and/

Katherine: *(Eyes closed)* The children are all asleep.

Jim: The children are all asleep. Under a spell. Happy dreams until Tuesday.

Katherine: When they wake up whatever they dream will be piled up the bed beside them.

Jim: Sweets.

Katherine: Thick as leaves.

Jim: *(He has stopped her by the armchair, locked the two brakes)* Now.

Katherine: And there's a cure for me.

Jim: *(Softly)* Kate. *(Pause. The grief locks them a moment)*

Katherine: *(Very quietly)* And I will go see the children. Go to Africa and America and/

Jim: Please Kate.

Katherine: Clap my hands and hold my own food and/

Jim: Don't.

Katherine: Dance!

She falls silent. A long moment. He has nothing to say. It is an awkward few beats before she can recover herself.

Katherine: Be a good time for the phone to ring.

Jim: They're bringing one back tomorrow.

Katherine: And taking me to the museum.

Jim: Stop.

Katherine: Sorry. Must be the poison working.

Jim: That's it. Very likely. *(Suddenly remembers, smiles)* There's a mobile one left somewhere. Until they bring tomorrow's. We're to have the special old-fashioned one, brass bits and things, for retirement. So he said. Took out the switch into the van, came back in, took one look at the pair of us and, mobile, he says. Mobile. *(Broken laugh)*

Katherine: *(Laughs)* You thought he was talking about me.

Jim: I didn't know what the hell. It was the way he said it. A little beauty you could have now, he said.

Katherine: D'you tell him you had a big beauty already?

Jim: Mobile. Cordless. Like that. No getting up getting down. Attach it to the chair says he, and you're connected.

Katherine: Calls on wheels.

Jim: Like strapping the switch to your back, I says to him. *(Half-laugh)* I think he thought I was beyond it/

Katherine: You are/

Jim: *(Taking the wheelchair)* Now where do you want to be?

Katherine: Africa.

Jim: Here or in the room?

Katherine: I suppose … this isn't America is it?

Jim: Hard to tell.

Katherine: Where are you going to be?

Jim: I'm going to be here. I had this idea that on the first night in forty years with no calls coming through here I might chance reading the paper. They say it's something to experience if you get to start at the first page and go right through to the last in one sitting. I wouldn't know myself.

Katherine: Well that's some … *(Slurs, then very clearly, angry at herself)* something I'd like to see.

Jim: *(Uncertain)* You'll sit here so?

Katherine: *(Very precisely)* I suppose I will.

Jim: All right.

*He tries to lift **Katherine** out of the wheelchair. It takes effort and he struggles. When at last he is holding her upright, suddenly she pushes herself back against him. He staggers and then falls to the floor and she falls on top of him. He cushions her but it is a serious fall. They are lying amidst the million sweet wrappers. A long moment. He is motionless beneath her, she is crying.*

Katherine: Jim! Jim. O. *(She tries to move her head, cries out)* Agh! O God Jim? *(No reaction, she tries to slide herself over)* Can you hear me? *(She is alongside him now but cannot reach with her hand)* Jim, Jim? *(Pause)* Please wake up, Jimmy? *(He opens his eyes, lies still)*

Katherine: Jimmy?

Jim: *(After a beat, quiet and calm)* Mary?

Katherine: *(Cry of dismay)* Stop! Stop that. Look, look at me, look at me. *(She wiggles on the floor to try and face him)* Shite! *(Tries to hit him)* Jim!

Jim: *(Coming to himself)* Agh, Kate.

Katherine: *(Lies her head beside him, is deeply wounded, softly)* Yes, Kate.

Jim: I … I … *(Whispers)* I'm sorry.

***Jim** tries to move around on the floor but can't. Cries out in pain.*

Jim: Oh God, I think my hip is broken. Agh!

*They lie there a long moment. No help is at hand, then through the door comes **Francis** with a suitcase. **Katherine** sees him.*

Katherine: Francis! Francis!

But when he steps in the door he just stands there a moment, and then **Ger** *comes in the door with her suitcase. She steps to the other side. A moment later* **Nora** *comes in breathlessly, carrying a duffle bag.*

Nora: Well, here we are!

Francis: Here we are.

Ger: Here we all are.

They stand. Nothing moves. Blackout.

END ACT ONE

ACT TWO

Lights come up on **Nora** *and* **Francis** *dancing to 'The Continental . They are mimics of* **Jimmy** *and* **Kate** *in Act One.* **Ger** *is sitting at the switch.* **Katherine** *is sitting in the swing. As the dance ends* **Nora** *and* **Francis** *come off into imaginary 'wings while the next act goes on.*

Francis: *(Playing* **Jimmy**, *holding* **Nora** *at arm s length)* Fabulous! God Kate, we were fabulous.

Nora: *(Playing* **Kate***)*: I was I suppose.

Francis: *(Laughs)* We've won again.

Nora: Of course we have. Who was there to beat us? The McInerney Family Singers?

Francis: 'The gypsy rover came over …'

Nora: Shsh Jimmy. They'll hear you. They're just over there!

Francis: *(Twirling her)* I don't care. I'm the happiest man in Clare when I'm dancing with you, do you know that?

Katherine: That's what he said.

Francis: *(Not interacting with her)* I'm the happiest man in Clare when I'm dancing with you.

Nora: *(Mimes fanning her face)* It's the usual effect I have.

Francis: O is it now?

Nora: So my lovers tell me.

Francis: That a fact? How many of them, or would that be ungentlemanly of me to ask the lady?

Katherine: Dozens.

Nora: Dozens. Who counts?

Francis: I see. Well let me tell you something/

Nora: Yes?/

Ger: Put your arms around her.

Francis: *(Arms encircling **Nora**)* None of them feel like I do. You're wonderful. You have me spinning like a top, dancing on the moon/

Nora: Is that where you were that last number?

Francis: "Like the drip drip drip of the raindrops when the summer shower is through, so a voice within me keeps repeating 'you you you …'"

Katherine: We don't have conversations do we?

Nora: I saw a few out there wanting conversation with you this evening.

Francis: *(Fake disbelief)* I'm sure you did. *(A beat)* Who?

Nora: Helen Igoe for one. Not that you'd go for her.

Francis: No go Igoe.

Nora: Face on her like prunes in custard.

Francis: I like custard.

Nora: Moira Mac.

Francis: That saint?

Nora: She had the eye tonight.

Francis: I prefer women with two.

Nora: Even old Monica was taking a shine.

Francis: There I was thinking I was polished enough.

Nora: I'm telling you/

Francis: *(Too abruptly)* Will you stop? Will you stop that? Are you trying to ruin everything?

Nora: *(Feeling the sharpness of his tone)* I was joking.

Francis: I know, but.

Nora: *(Looking away)* All right so.

Pause.

Francis: *(Drawing out a sweet, holds it in front of her)* Turkish delight? *(She lets it dangle there for a time)*

Nora: Are you insisting?

Francis: I am.

Nora: *(Takes it, still with her back to him)* You grow these, don't you? That's what I will advise the girls.

Katherine and Nora: Marry a man with an everlasting supply of sweetness.

Francis: I'm going to leave you for a minute and go up the street and check the children, see that Mary's all right on the switch. I'll be back before the prizes. Are you all right?

Katherine: Just watch out for Moira Mac.

*He half-laughs and leaves. She stands there while he crosses the stage hurriedly, going up the street and coming in to where **Ger** is sitting at the switch.*

Francis: Mary!

Ger: I thought you'd forgotten me Jimmy.

*The moment he comes in the door she is in his arms and they are embracing passionately. Haste, passion, then, **Nora** steps forward* *as herself aged five, picking up her blanket, and stands watching and says:*

Nora: Daddy?

Abruptly the scene explodes. **Katherine** *cries out.* **Francis** *goes up into the tree. The light finds him.*

Katherine: Francis?

Francis: *(Waits, tries to regain himself to carry on lecture)* Can it be so? We ask ourselves in atomic physics if the human observer is in fact a necessary feature, for if the properties of an object are not observed how can they be defined as existing? They cannot. All is part of the whole, the inter-dynamic energy. I quote Heisenberg: 'What we observe is not nature itself, but nature exposed to our method of questioning.' This implies then a relation which is crucial to our understanding; that we are the interpreters of this relation/

Katherine: Francis?

Francis: *(Disturbed, but carrying on)* ... has been taken by some to mean that ... we can also be regarded ... as its ... creators too.

Katherine: *(Softly)* It wasn't like that.

Francis: A fantasy ...

Katherine: It wasn't like that.

Francis: *(Not turning towards her)* I can't hear you. You're not here.

Katherine: He never left me then.

Francis: *(Walking away)* I can't hear you. I'm not listening.

Katherine: Not when I was well. It wasn't like that.

Francis: *(Cries out in frustration)* Stop. Stop it!

Katherine: Francis?

Francis: I can't. I can't. You're not even here. You're there.

Katherine: I'm here.

Francis: This is a dream. I'm dreaming of you.

Katherine: And I'm here. I'm always here.

Francis: O God! This is Berkeley, this is California. I'm a physics lecturer/

Katherine: It's very nice.

Francis: You're not here. You can't even walk.

Katherine: Magic carpet.

Francis: You're at home, you're in the post office, you're stuck there, sitting there with him, old dancing ears.

Katherine: My lover.

Francis: O God, I don't believe this. This isn't happening. You're not here. *(He walks away then turns, looks at her)*

Katherine: I am here for your grief.

Francis: It's make believe. The whole thing was. No basis in reality. That's the trouble. Our whole childhood was make believe. Make believe we had this glamorous dancing mammy and daddy, this pair of dancing Dooleys and everything was hunky-dorey and rosy in the garden; and all the time it was …

Katherine: He loves me.

Francis: *(Turning away)* You're not here I can't talk to you.

Katherine: You love me. All of you do.

Francis: That's why we all left.

Katherine: You haven't left. None of you have. Didn't I teach you anything? Francie? We all fly in and out of each other, remember that?

Francis: You're dying. You've been dying since I was twelve years old. Little by little.

Katherine: We can be anything we want, anywhere we want. You know that. *(She steps to him)*

Francis: First you couldn't walk, then you/

Katherine: Come on. *(Reaches out a hand he does not see)*

Francis: You couldn't …

Katherine: Come on Francie. We're in the garden.

Francis: I'm in California.

Katherine: *(Closes her eyes, holds out her hand to him)* We're in the garden playing.

Francis: I'm a physics lecturer.

Katherine: Shsh. All space is the same space when there's love in it. Francis. Come on. Wings? *(Arms outstretched)* We're flying. We're flying. Ger is best. You're behind me. Nora's nervous. Round the whitethorn when the blossoms have fallen.

*And for a moment **Ger** and **Nora** are there too, arms out, standing motionlessly flying.*

Katherine: We're all together, though we're not. Come on Francis, come on. Close your eyes. You're there.

He closes his eyes, hugs himself.

Francis: You're not here.

Katherine: I am here.

Francis: You're there. You can't move.

Katherine: I can fly. I taught all my children to fly. Come on. Francis! Let it go.

At last he holds wide his arms, gradually joining the others. The stillness of mother and children standing there holds a few moments and then is broken suddenly as the lights come up brightly and **Jimmy** *comes flying out the garden playfully shooting dak-dak machine guns as he swoops among them. Throughout the following* **Nora** *should be somewhat wary of her father and close to* **Kate**. *It becomes clear* **Jimmy** *is trying hard to be having fun with them, not quite bridging an earlier coolness with* **Kate**.

Jimmy: Dak-dak-dak-dak-dak.

Ger: *(Falls to the ground)* Aghgh! I'm wounded!

Kate: *(Collapsing, laugh)* Oh I think he got me!

Nora: *(Staying close to and copying mother)* Me too!

Francis: *(Falling, shooting* **Jim** *as he does)* Dak-dak-dak, AH!

Jimmy: You got me!

They all fall in a happy heap on the ground.

Ger: Mind your foot!

Kate: Whose hand is this?

Francis: Agh I'm bleeding.

Nora: So am I.

Ger: I've lost my arms.

Jimmy: I've lost my heart. Where is it, where is it? *(Pretend scrambling / searching)*

Ger: *(Offering the sweet wrapper-leaves)* Here, here it is Daddy.

Jimmy: Ah thank you Flight Officer Dooley. Any one seen a parachuting blonde coming down?

Ger: Was it me?

Jimmy: Ah. Sorry, no me love. A bigger woman. *(His joke not taken, cold glance from **Kate**)* But not very big.

Francis: *(Holding up his mother's head)* Could this be her?

Jimmy: *(Looks)* No, sorry, not big enough. I mean yes, perfect, that's her all right. How are you dear, Flight Officer Dear?

Nora: She's Dooley.

Jimmy: Dear Dooley?

Kate: I might recover *(To **Nora**)* with a kiss.

***Nora** kisses her and with a cry they all kiss her, and she calls out.*

Kate: Enough, enough! I'm all better, thank you.

Jimmy: *(Lying there with them)* Well, looks pretty bad from here.

Nora: *(On the point of sudden tears)* Mammy.

Kate: Shsh Nora. It's not too bad at all. It's only pretend.

Ger: No it's not. It's terrible.

Francis: We've all broken our legs and can't get away. We can't move.

Ger: And there's natives coming.

Francis: They're going to eat us!

Nora: *(Alarmed)* Ah!

Kate: No they're not. We're going to charm them. Aren't we?

Francis: We have to put a spell on them! Like wizards!

Ger: We can make them vanish.

Jimmy: *(Taps the floor)* Shsh! I think I hear drums!

Kate: *(Taps too with **Nora**)* O my God, they're coming.

Ger: They're coming!

Francis: Ready with the spell!

Nora: What is it? I don't know it!

Ger: It's/

Kate: *(After a beat, begins mad-quick singing)* The Continental! The Continental!

They all join in, mad-fast kick line from their lying-down position on the floor. From off-stage the switch begins to ring.

Francis: They're going away!

Ger: They're going! And I'm cured! *(She stands up)*

Francis: *(Standing)* Me too! I can fly again! *(Arms go out)*

Kate: The switch! Shsh, it's ringing!

Ger: *(Groans)* Aw! It always ruins it.

Nora: *(Getting up)* I'll get it! Can I? Can I?

Jimmy: Go on then, quick!

*****Nora*** goes off to answer it. **Francis** and **Ger** step to either side of the two parents who are now lying there on the floor in the position of the end of Act One. The two children have their arms wide like planes and are looking away from the parents. **Ger** lowers her* *arms, **Francis** in California, his mother/dream vanished. The switch ringing stops when **Francis** in America answers the phone call from Africa.*

Nora: Caherconn hello?

Francis: Hello?

Ger: Francis, it's me.

Francis: Ger, Jesus. I can hardly hear you. Where are you?

Ger: I'm in Niarobi. I just spoke to Nora.

Francis: How are you?

Ger: Great! I'm great. How are you?

Francis: How am I? How am I? God what a terrible question.

Ger: What's the matter Francie?

Francis: I can't define it. I can't seem to … I don't know. Anyway it doesn't matter.

Ger: Do you know they closed the switch today?

Francis: Yes.

Ger: Nora's going down.

Francis: You think I should go home.

Ger: What?

Francis: Do you think … You do think that I should go home. Don't you? Nora thinks it but says she won't be the one to tell anyone what to do. She's only the younger sister.

Ger: *(Half-laugh)* That's Nora all right. The bossiest of all of us.

Francis: Do you think about her?

Ger: Nora?

Francis: Mam. I do, I think about her all the time. Some days I can't get her out of my head. Like she's right here in the room with me.

Ger: That's handy.

Francis: Ger.

Ger: Well, saves you going home.

Francis: You know what I mean. It's, I know it's nothing anyone is interested in or thinks about except me, but it's, it's like/

Ger: Go on.

Francis: /like we're particles/

Ger: Particles? Us?

Francis: /communicating across a void in a way that no science can prove possible. As if we defy space and time and gravity and all the rest of it.

Ger: You've lost me.

Francis: I know. No, it doesn't matter.

Ger: I don't know what to say. She's with Dad. And I know what you think, but he's taking care of her. He's looking after her every day. He's her husband. You could forgive him maybe.

Francis: *(Pause)* Do you?

Ger: Don't ask me. I'm in and out of love every ten days. I can't answer for Dad. I can't answer for you, I can't answer for Nora.

Francis: Will you go home?

Ger: I don't know. I love it out here. I feel so free. I can go whole days and not think once about it. What does that make me in particles? The selfish molecule? I care. Of course I care. Nora thinks because I'm a nurse I should be there, because I'm not the one married with kids.

Francis: We grew up in a make-believe, you know that?

Ger: It was wonderful.

Francis: Dancing Mam and Dad. We had no idea of what the real world was like. We thought it was all moonlight and stars, prizes and chocolates and roses.

Ger: It is.

Francis: What?

Ger: Sometimes it is.

Francis: I can't hear you. Ger? Ger?

She is gone. **Francis** *sits in the tree.* **Nora** *runs out to her parents who are lying on the floor from the game.*

Nora: I did it. I put the call through.

Jimmy: Good girl.

Nora: Where are the others gone?

Kate: They're gone down the garden somewhere I think.

Jimmy: Left your Mam and Dad stuck here. Give us a hand up Nora? *(He reaches up to her; she is awkward about taking his hand, but does. He lets her imagine she is pulling him up)* Good girl, look at the strength of that girl! *(As he stands)* Now your Mam.

Kate: That's a bigger job. Oh! Oh! *(Rising on **Nora** s pull)* Yes! Yes, she's up! Thank you Nora.

Nora: You're welcome Mammy.

Jimmy: Best girl, aren't you? *(She says nothing)* Now run down and find the others and tell them come up in fifteen minutes for chops and onions. Go on!

Nora: Will you come with me Mammy?

Kate: Who's going to cook the dinner?

Nora: Can I come in and help?

Jimmy: Go on down the garden. They'll be waiting for you.

Nora: Mammy?

Kate: Go on pet, you'll be back in a minute.

She runs off. **Jimmy** *and* **Kate** *walk slowly back into the house. There is a coolness between them. She goes and picks up the paper he has dropped on the floor, he goes to the switch. It is some moments before they speak.*

Kate: You don't usually come out.

Jimmy: Well.

Kate: I thought you didn't approve.

Jimmy: Not all the time. That's all I said, not all the time that kind of carry-on, they're older, Francis and Ger too, going round pretending all the time. That's all I said. Makes them …

Kate: What?

Jimmy: Nothing. It was just a thing I said. That's all.

Pause.

Kate: Are we going to talk about it?

Jimmy: What?

Kate: You know what.

Jimmy: O God Kate.

Kate: Don't 'Oh God' me. Tell me.

Jimmy: What do you want me to say?

Kate: I want you to say you didn't look sideways at her. I want you to say if you did it was her ugly nose, her crooked mouth, the great big birthmark on her neck you were just thinking was a map of China, that that was what you were thinking.

Jimmy: You're going crazy on me.

Kate: I am.

Jimmy: God's sake.

Kate: You're not telling me.

Jimmy: What? I don't care tuppence about her. She was, I was/

Kate: Looking at her.

Jimmy: I am not going to talk about it. You imagine everything. You imagine so much you can't tell the difference between things. You've the children the same.

Kate: Leave them out of it. This isn't about them. It's about/

Jimmy: I left you for ten minutes! Ten minutes in the name of …

Kate: Yes, ten minutes. How was I to know where you were?

Jimmy: Checking on the children. Walking up the street by myself to come in here and see were they all right? Were they asleep? That's where I was. I went because you had finished telling me earlier how Nora was always clinging on to you now. How the three of them were like tied on to you now and you hadn't a moment when you didn't feel there weren't three wires running out of them into your chest. I went to save you going. Not for anything else. Now. Take your imaginings away into some book or something.

Kate: You left me.

Jimmy: I/

Kate: You left me. That's what I was thinking.

Jimmy: All right. All right I'm sorry. I told you/

Kate: It's all right. I was just upset that's all.

Pause.

Jimmy: Well?

Kate: What?

Jimmy: Will I cook the chops?

A beat, she doesn t answer.

Kate: Do you think it's one special moment when a man stops seeing a woman as beautiful?

Jimmy: Jesus Kate. I'm not listening to you.

Kate: Stops him even listening to her?

Jimmy: Stop it.

Kate: The same as the one when he falls in love. When he sees her. Might have seen her for months beforehand and never took much notice. Mellie Hayes and Paddy Ryan say.

Jimmy: What about them?

Kate: Buying groceries in the same place, meeting ten years and then, one day he sees her: the way she looks/

Jimmy: *(Moving)* I'm going to cook the chops.

Kate: That's a moment, isn't it?

Jimmy: *(Stands)* Yes, of course it's/

Kate: *(Increasingly upset, onto bitter tears)* So, it makes perfect sense doesn't it? Another moment when fzzz, like that, it just fizzles out, the live wire, connection, and there's nothing she can do about it, she's just left standing there, feeling how all of a sudden she's very thick around the hips, and her legs aren't that shapely anymore and she's got another part of her chin that she never had before, and her skin is suddenly very dry, very very dry, and it's true she can't wear the dress she used to, the black silk dress with the golden bow he tied up at her back, because the spell is coming off, O O Cinderella get home, the spell is coming off, you're turning into somebody not beautiful any more, you're becoming/

Jimmy: *(Moving to her, grief welling)* Kate.

Kate: *(Weeping)* Ugly.

Jimmy: *(Arms going around her)* You're not/

Kate: I am. I know I am.

Jimmy: Kate. You're/

Kate: And that's why you can't think I'm/

Jimmy: Stop! Stop talking.

Kate: That's the answer. Stop talking start dancing. Keep dancing and make believe it's/

Jimmy: Please Kate. Please.

Kate: Not happening. That's what I kept telling myself, standing there last night waiting for you to come back. I thought what if he doesn't come back/

Jimmy: I wouldn't/

Kate: What if he doesn't? And you didn't. He's gone from me now I thought, and sure why wouldn't he? Look at me, I'm not. I'm. In the light. See me in the light and you can see the old woman creeping up on me. Getting into my skin.

Jimmy: Kate. *(He holds her)*

Kate: I'm/

Jimmy: Stop!

A moment.

Kate: *(Sudden alarm)* Jim O I'm dizzy. I'm dizzy. I feel like everything's turning.

Jimmy: Here, hold onto me, come on. *(He moves her)* You need to lie down, you're/

Kate: My legs are full of pins and needles! *Jim*!

Jimmy: Easy now, easy love.

He is holding her up when **Nora** *returns from the garden without the others. When she sees* **Jimmy** *dragging off her mother she has a hysterical fit, and thinks that he has hurt her.*

Nora: Mammy? *(Shouts)* Mammy?

Jimmy: Leave her, Nora, leave her alone.

Nora: Mammy what's happened? Mammy why/

Jimmy: Quiet will you?

Nora: *(Throws herself on her father, pummelling him)* You, you hurt …

Jimmy: Stop it Nora! Stop it!

*She continues to hit him. One-handed, he pushes her off him roughly and then goes to take **Kate** off. He acts as if he does, but **Kate** stays and watches **Nora** whimpering.*

Nora: *(Quietly)* I hate you! I hate you! Hate hate hate hate you! *(She sinks to the floor and hugs her knees)* I'm going to run away. I'm going to run away and never come back. I'm going to go with Ger and Francie and Mammy and never come back. We're going to join a circus and be flying trapeze clowns and be the funniest best ones, the funniest best ones in the whole circus. Everybody will be laughing at us cause of all the funny things. And we'll go places. Together. We'll go everywhere there is to go.

Katherine: Three times.

Nora: Three times. Francie and Ger and Mammy and Me, and we'll have magic carpets that fly away and never fly back. We'll eat turkish delights and ice cream all the time and not get sick.

Katherine: Never get sick.

Nora: We'll never get sick. And we'll all be together cause we'll put a magic string tying between us so we can never ever be apart, ever, and cause I'm the youngest … I get to say where we go first.

*She starts to turn about holding her knees, going around and around. **Jimmy** now in his suit and dancing shoes comes out. He calls back to the room off-stage.*

Jimmy: I'm going now. All right? Bye! *(Nothing)*

Katherine: *(Weakly)* Bye.

*And he is gone. He moves to the back, upstage. The music of Fred Astaire comes up and he starts to dance, in low light. This continues throughout the following as **Katherine** sits softly into her wheelchair and suddenly there is a burst of giggles, whoops, and laughter as **Francis** and **Ger** instantly appear and race their mother out on her new wheelchair. She is new to it, her hands are not yet affected by the illness. The mood is wild and jubilant.*

Francis: *(As he heads for **Nora**)* A rock! A rock!

Ger: Watch out!

Katherine: *(In warning)* Nora!

Nora: Help! *(She jumps up)*

Francis: Climb aboard! *(Turning the wheelchair sharply with all three children now behind it)* All aboard Spaceship Mother!

Ger: Aye-aye.

Katherine: Don't crash her whatever you do.

Francis: Have no fears/

Katherine: She's the only Spaceship Mother you've got.

Nora: *(Hugs her)* I love her. She's the best.

Ger: Alright now, where to?

Francis: Mars!

Ger: Venus!

Nora: The moon!

Francis: The moon it is! Stand by!

Ger: Stand by!

They zoom their mother along and around in a circle.

Katherine: Careful! I'm flying off!

Francis: Hang on!

Ger: Watch out!

They twirl her around and cry out before 'landing at her feet.

Katherine: *(Opening her eyes)* Are we here?

Nora: *(Closing hers)* Yes. Look.

Ger and Francis close their eyes.

Francis: Yes!

Ger: It's lovely. The moon is so lovely.

A moment in which Katherine is looking at them, suddenly struck.

Katherine: Do you know, the three of you are the most wonderful children in the world. I wish you would never grow up.

Francis: *(Eyes closed, arms out pretends to float)* Shsh. We're on the moon.

Ger: *(Copying him)* Yes.

Francis: You know why we came here?

Katherine: Why?

Francis: Because you don't need your wheelchair. Because you can float in the air.

Nora: Because Daddy's not here.

Katherine: Nora. That's not nice.

Nora: I don't want him to be here.

Ger: He didn't want to be anyway. He went out dancing.

Katherine: Because I wanted him to. He asked me. I told him to go. Do you think it's fair Daddy should stay home all the time and mind me just because now I can't go out?

Francis: Shsh. I'm on the moon.

Katherine: It wouldn't be fair.

The children are ignoring her. Moon-exploring.

Katherine: It wouldn't be. Daddy's a wonderful dancer. He's got ... all these dancing bits inside him. The way he's made, it's ... like flashing shiny pieces of ... when he's dancing everything is brilliant and bright, and it's ... He has to dance. He has to. (**Nora** *comes to her feet and she looks at her softly)* I want him to. I do. *(Takes **Nora** s hand)* Besides, we can all be together. And we don't need any old Mary on the switch, we can handle it ourselves. And. And!, it's the only time now we can play like this. *(Fake authority)* Because you're all getting too old for games.

Nora: Not me.

Francis: *(Moon-exploring)* I've found something!

Ger: What is it? Let me see!

Katherine: Quick, let Spaceship Mother see!

Nora *pushes her over.*

Nora: What is it?

Katherine: Francis?

Francis: It's space medicine.

Ger: Great!

Nora: It's for Mammy.

Ger: It's full of moon.

Francis: *(Holds it up in his hands)* Here it is.

Ger: It'll make you better.

Nora: You'll walk.

Katherine: No. I won't. Nora pet. I/

Francis: Please mammy.

She takes it, stillness. The children look up at her as if for a moment it might really work. **Katherine** *lowers her head, is about to weep.*

Katherine: *(Whisper)* I'm sorry.

A lost moment, no magic, then **Francis**, **Ger** *and* **Nora** *reach under their mother and together slowly lift her into the air.*

Katherine: Don't! Francis, children, wait, you'll/

Francis: Shush, don't. See, it works!

Nora: It works!

Ger: You're in the air/

Francis: On the moon! There's less gravity, see.

Katherine: You'll drop me!

Francis: We're not even touching you.

Nora: It's the moon medicine.

Katherine: Put me down now, Francis, Ger.

They move with her across the moon; the light is white and wonderful; it is like a dance and there is no fear of her falling.

Katherine: Back in my chair. Now, please.

Ger: That's the spaceship.

Katherine: I'm too heavy.

Francis: You're not heavy in space.

Nora: *(Struggling to hold her up)* You're light as a feather.

Katherine: Put me down, now, that's an order.

Francis: I'm the captain.

Ger: We're going around the moon.

Katherine: *(As they lower her legs to the ground, supporting her between them)* Please! In my chair.

Nora: You can walk!

Katherine: I can't!

Nora: You can Mammy, you can!

Jimmy enters the post office, returning from the dance. The moment he appears the light hardens. He stands and sees Katherine held now in a position as if she can walk again, the children behind her propping her up; illusionary moment of miracle.

Jimmy: *(Joy)* O God! You're walking!

He rushes to her, the children step back and vanish and she falls forward heavily into his arms, knocking him to the floor amidst cries of anguish and hurt. And the light now returns us to the position at the end of Act One with Katherine and Jim crying out on the floor. Returning to the moment of the end of Act One, Francis and Ger and Nora come in turns through the door. The moment should seem hopeful; help has arrived; but for an instant only. Katherine sees the dream-figures, Jim passes out. The children do not react to their mother.

Ger: Well, here we are.

Katherine: Francis? Francis? Nora?

Nora: We've run away.

Katherine: Ger? Help me!

Nora: We've run away from home and we're never going back.

Francis: We'll go back to get Mammy. When our house is made.

Ger: It'll be really nice.

Nora: Not like at home.

Francis: Home is nice.

Nora: I don't like it anymore. I don't want to be there. I don't. I don't.

Ger: Shsh, Nora, quiet. It's alright. We're not going back, we've come here — see.

Francis: We're just us.

Ger: Free of everybody. *(Dances a step)* See, nothing holding on to us. Just brother and sisters. We can go anywhere. Come on. *(She leads them in hand-held circles around the room)*

Katherine: Ger? Help. Help! Francis, Nora?

The children stop and sit in tribunal.

Nora: Daddy loves Mary Mulvihill.

Ger: And Mrs. Mac.

Francis: And Maggie Crimmins.

Ger: Joanie Fitz says he loves her Mammy too. Says she saw them dancing together really close in Dalys on Sunday. She says her Daddy's going to kill ours when he finds out. Kill him with a knife. Cut off his thing, that's what she said.

Nora: Ugh!

Francis: He won't.

Ger: He might.

Francis: I'm going to tell Mammy.

Ger: You can't.

Nora: Yes you can.

Ger: No you can't. What's the good of that? That's not any good, she'll cry. You'll only hurt her more. Daddy says Mammy can't be upset. We're not to upset her. Makes her sickness worse.

Francis: She is not getting better anyway.

Nora: Yes she is. She's going to.

Francis: No she's not. She's not Nora. She's going to get worse. Tell her Ger, tell her what you heard the doctor say.

Ger: Mammy's not going to get better Nora. She's never going to walk again.

Francis: And it's going to reach out more and more, she's not going to be able to move anything, and then she's/

Nora: Daddy did it! Daddy did it to her.

Ger: No he didn't.

Nora: Yes he did. She was fine until, until/

Francis: I hate him! I hate him, I hate him, I'm going to kill him first!

Nora: I am too.

Ger: You can't. You don't/

Francis: Everybody in school's laughing at him. They say things. I know they do. They're whispering in the corner of the yard. I hit Tommy Clancy for it.

Nora: You shouldn't be taking his side. I wouldn't. I'm going to tell Mammy and she'll leave him and run away with us.

Ger: She won't.

Nora: Yes she will.

Ger: She won't.

Katherine: *(Whisper)* I won't.

Ger: Because she loves him.

Katherine: *(Whisper)* Because I love him.

Francis: You're wrong.

Ger: No I'm not.

Francis: *(Gathering intensity)* You're wrong, you're wrong you're wrong! She doesn't. She doesn't. She used to. But not when we tell her. Then she won't.

Ger: We can't tell her.

Francis: Yes we can.

Nora: Everybody who comes in the post office knows. Everybody!

Francis: Dancey Pants! That's what they call him! Dancey Pants Dooley! And he thinks it's all a big secret, all his big secret! He thinks he knows everything in the village, he thinks he hears everything that's going on and that nobody knows about him. He thinks nobody knows when he goes out. Dancey pants, dancey pants!

Ger: Stop it Francis. Stop it. *(Pause)* We can't tell her. It would break her heart.

Nora: What can we do then? I don't want to live here anymore. I don't like it. *(Getting more upset)* I don't like everybody laughing at me.

Ger: *(Comforting her)* Shsh Nora, don't cry.

Nora: I'm never going to marry anybody.

Francis: Me neither.

Nora: I'm going to be a nun.

Francis: I'm going to fly spaceships and see far planets and never go to dances.

Ger: I am. I'm going to fall in love. One time, forever. And he's never going to love anyone else but me.

Nora: Then you should be a nun. 'Cause nobody else will. Nobody will/

Ger: Love only me? He will.

Francis: Tommy Eyres.

Ger: What?

Francis: I know.

Ger: I never said anything about Tommy Eyres.

Francis: Or Marty Keane.

Nora: Him?

Ger: I only ever spoke to him once, to ask him for a pencil.

Francis: Mickey Mac says you're in love with him. It's written on the wall at the back of the shed.

Ger: Must be himself wrote it.

Francis: That's not what I heard.

Ger: Shut up you.

Francis: I'm only repeating what/

Ger: Shut up! Do you hear me? Do you? *(He is wounded, she goes toward him, then gestures* **Nora** *to the two of them)* We're to stick together. We're to stick together and not fight and be the best brother and sisters to each other ever and always.

Francis turns slowly away, moving into adulthood and the tree space that is California, even as **Nora** *and* **Ger** *return to the spaces that are Leitrim and Africa. As he does, the carpet that* **Katherine** *and* **Jim** *are lying on rises from the back and tilts upright until it reaches an angle and we seem to be looking down on them.*

Francis: None of us will ever love anybody right, now. Not ourselves, and not others. How can you believe in anything when you find out your mother and father were just made up? Love a fairytale. *(He is at his chair)* Our fault too. None of us letting it out of the bag year after year until we grew used to not seeing it, to going around with our ears shut and our eyes shut, the blind deaf Dooley children. Each of us pulling down the blinds so that we could eventually walk out the post office door and leave her there without too much guilt. Mother/

Ger: *(In swing)* I have to go, I've got a job in Africa.

Francis: /Mother I've got a lectureship; it's physics, it's in California. Mother/

Nora: I'm pregnant, I'm going to marry Paddy Blake. He's from Leitrim.

Francis: One year, all three of us, blind mice, gone.

Katherine: Jim? Jim? Wake up!

Jim: *(Rousing back to pain)* Oh, what? What? O!

Katherine: Are you all right? You passed out. Jim?

Jim: *(Coming to)* O God.

Katherine: What is it?

Jim: Agh! My hip, I think it's ... O! I've broken my hip.

Katherine: Don't say that.

Jim: I have. It's, O God! Jesus!

Katherine: O Jim.

He scrambles around with difficulty to reach down to his legs.

Jim: I can't feel my legs. Kate! Kate I can't feel my legs!

A moment, then she bursts out laughing.

Jim: What? What is it? What are you laughing at?

Katherine: I can't feel mine either.

Jim: It's not funny. Ow!

Katherine: *(Still laughing)* It's hysterical.

Jim: Stop it. Did you hear me? I think my hip's broken.

Katherine: I'm sure it is.

Jim: What? I can't get up.

Katherine: I know. Isn't it funny?

Jim: It's ... Did you hit your head?

Katherine: Want to dance?

Jim: Are you in your right mind? I've broken my hip. I'm not joking, I can't move on my o—/

Katherine: Don't move. Stay absolutely still. Do you hear me? Now, we can talk.

Jim: Talk? What are you/

Katherine: Stay still; I can't get up, you can't get up. Neither of us are going anywhere.

Jim: This isn't a game Kate, this isn't a joke, I'm after/

Katherine: I know, I know you are. Lie still, deep breath. Now.

Jim: Now what?

Katherine: *(Catches breath)* Well, here we are! Here we all are.

Jim: You're happy you knocked me over and landed on top of me and broke my hip? Is that it?

Katherine: I wasn't sure I would break your hip. I thought maybe a leg.

Jim: What?

Katherine: I wasn't sure. I thought maybe you'd be knocked out.

Jim: What are you saying?

Katherine: Then I wouldn't be able to talk to you.

Jim: You wanted to knock me over?

Katherine: I did. A leg would have been okay.

Jim: You wanted to break my leg?

Katherine: Would any wife want less.

Jim: I don't follow a thing you're saying. I'm not even listening to you.

Katherine: This is when you walk away. This is when you go into the kitchen and pour yourself a drink, and I sit here waiting for you to come back. *(Pause)* But you won't come back until you're sure I won't say anything again. Now, there you are.

Jim: You ought to be locked up.

Katherine: I am. Everyday.

Jim: That's not what I meant.

Katherine: It's what I meant. *(Pause)* Please Jim, listen. I wanted to talk to you. To talk to you when you couldn't walk away.

Jim: I don't walk away, I take good care of you.

Katherine: I know you do.

Jim: I get you dressed, I pick you up and put you down. I wash your things, I rub the food stains out of your blouses, I do all that.

Katherine: You do and I'll tell you why. I'll tell you what I thought sitting here in the chair. I thought it's guilt not love. All that. That's what it is. It's so many dinners cooked and fed equals an evening out with Moira Mac.

Jim: No Kate.

Kate: Shut up Jim. Bringing me tea five times a day equals the freedom to walk away? To leave me here while you're click-clacking away in Daly's and shining the moon and stars for someone else. I know Jim. I know. I heard it on the switch. I heard Maggie Keane talking about you, how you were a walking scandal. And I sat there listening. It was like hearing a story about somebody else, someone not you. Not my Jimmy. My man in love with Mary Mulvihill. My man dancing with Moira Mac. *(Pause)* I don't blame you. Look at me, old tub of turkish delight.

Jim: Kate, you're still beautiful.

Katherine: Stop. Don't! Don't. I don't want to hear it. I don't want to pretend now. I've been doing that for thirteen years Jim. I've been sitting there in that bloody chair watching my husband dance around the parish with other women and I think I'm entitled this one ti … ti … ti. Just this one *time* to get my bit said, to get the thing clear and out in the open. I want to say it out loud one time. Helen, and Maureen and Sheila. You've held them in your arms. You've stroked their hair like you've stroked mine and kissed their lips and moved with them across the floor like once you moved with me.

I know Jim. I wanted you to know that I know. I covered it up with dreams. Imagined my dashing Prince, imagined that of all the princesses in the world he still loved me the best. I was the one he secretly danced with when he was dancing with the others. I was the one in his mind when he was taking his shiny shoes down the stairs and out the post office door, closing me in with the children where I played Pretend.

I stayed Jim. I stayed and taught them how to grow wings and fly away. See how they flew? Away.

Jim: I/

Katherine: Of all the princesses in the world he came to me. I was the one he secretly danced with when he was dancing with the others, I was the one in his mind even when click-clack click-clack he took his shiny shoes down the stairs and out the street, closing me in the post office with the children coming to me to play pretend. Pretend he wasn't going off dancing with Mary Mulvihill. Pretend he wasn't kissing her, wasn't dancing her to my Persia, not to my secret place; I was there by myself with him, and sometimes with the prince and princess children that I was teaching to fly. What I wanted to do was teach them to grow wings; grow wings and you can fly anywhere and

away from anything. See how they flew Jim? They flew.
One after the other. Away from it. Because they knew too.
Fancey Dancey Pants. That's what they call you. Even
now, even old and even now, Dancey Pants the Postmaster.
My dancing man.

He is weeping.

Katherine: I heard it on the switch. But I knew already. I
heard Maggie Keane talk about you. How you were a
walking scandal. And I sat there listening. Imagine. Like
hearing a story about someone else, someone not you, and
yet knowing it was you. Of course it was you. My man in
love with Mary Mulvihill. My man dancing with Moira
Mac. When she came in for stamps I saw how she asked
you for them.

Jim: You never said. You/

Katherine: I flew away. Whenever I wanted. It was easy. I
flapped my wings and headed off. Deaf and blind and flying
away in my wheelchair until the children left. He'll come in
one morning and want to tell me, and I'll be dribbling on
my chin and needing a tissue and he'll look at me and think;
how can I leave her like that. Pity will keep him . He's too
good a man just to walk away/

Jim: It's not/

Katherine: But he'll want to. I'll be driving him off, a little
bit further every day. I've been testing it. See will he brush
my hair? Ask him to take me to the bathroom again. See,
will he do it? Does he love me still? Will he say feck off
Kate, you need a nurse. Go on drive him off, let him go.
And you're still not gone. Still there everyday, still picking
me up and putting me down; I know.

Jim: I'm not in/

Katherine: Shsh. Don't say anything. I knocked you down so you could listen. You old fool. I know it wasn't until, until this started. I know. Once I was here in the chair, when you knew I wasn't getting out of it, never going to dance with you again. That's when you started leaving me/

Jim: I didn't leave you/

Katherine: Not altogether. But gone all the same.

Jim: I/

Katherine: Don't. Please Jim. Listen to me. There is no one else calling, the switch is gone. There's just. Listen. I want you to say it. I want you to say it's all true.

Pause, he is turned away; she waits.

Katherine: Jim? Jim?

Jim: *(Whisper)* It's true.

Pause, a long moment.

Jim: I'm sorry Kate.

Katherine: Shush, don't.

Jim: I'm sorry.

Katherine: Stop Jim. My Jimmy. I don't want you to, you can't change thirteen years. Can't roll them back as I can't get up and dance away with you. That's not why. That's not what I wanted.

Jim: I'm a fool, a/

Katherine: You're my dancing man. You're my dashing moonlight and roses man, you're my sweet man.

Jim: I'm sorry, I'm sorry, I/

Katherine: Shush, don't. Jim, Jim, Please.

Jim: I'm a weak man. I couldn't help myself. It wasn't, it didn't even matter, it was …

Katherine: Shush. I'm not saying it for you to say anything. I don't want you to say a thing. When we stopped dancing, when I lay at home those nights and could hear the music, I could hear the music so clearly floating out on the street when the children were in bed, knowing they weren't sleeping either, all of us lying there in our covers, like fallen-down stars, hearing the music Daddy was dancing to. Dancing in the dark. Night and Day. I missed it so much, so much. I missed you/

Jim: You were there/

Katherine: I was not.

Jim: You were/

Katherine: In Mary Mulvihill's flowery old dress? In Moira Mac's fake fur? No I wasn't.

Jim: I knew you could hear it up the street.

Katherine: You did I suppose.

Jim: I knew. It wasn't that I stopped. I didn't stop/

Katherine: Leaving me/

Jim: Loving you.

Katherine: You stopped seeing me as woman. *(Pause)* And I don't blame you. But it killed me just the same. It killed the part of me that you wanted to dance with once. The parts of me that still wanted you to touch them, to make me feel I was more than just an illness. That wanted you so terribly not to leave her behind, that girl you kissed and touched and caressed and made feel so alive. But you left her. *(Pause)* Now I'm leaving you.

Jim: Kate.

Katherine: *(Half-laughing)* It's my turn. I want to go out dancing.

Jim: I'll take you. I'll bring/

Katherine: You can't come. That's what I wanted to tell you. I'm leaving you. I can feel it. I can hardly swallow. In the mornings I struggle to breathe. I have pains in my stomach, pains in every part of me I don't tell you about. After thirteen years it's finally caught up with me. I can feel the tap on my shoulder. I'm leaving you, I'm dying Jim.

Jim: We can take you to the doctor, you/

Katherine: Don't be silly. Don't. Shush. Lie there and listen to me. I should have knocked you down years ago. Should be in the marriage manual. Be still sweet man. Listen to me. *(Pause)* I forgive you.

Jim: Don't/

Katherine: I forgive you everything. And I want you to forgive me.

He is weeping.

Katherine: See. I always told you I was a big woman. Please don't cry Jim.

Jim: I don't want to go on without you. I'm sorry, I'm sorry, I'm sorry, I'm weak and stupid, and — *(Cries out)* Agh! If I wasn't so, so/

Katherine: Sweet/

Jim: None of this would have happened.

Katherine: Yes it would. It would have been worse. Much worse.

He drags himself around to her, evidently in pain.

Jim: I don't want you to die.

Katherine: It won't be so bad.

Jim: I don't want you to. Please. I want to be/

Katherine: I'll fly off.

Jim: Kate!

Katherine: Just like a twirl off your arm, spinning away. Must be fun. That's when I'll win trophies. Nobody like me for a foxtrot then, light as air. *(Hums a line of 'The Continental)* Da de dah dah dah!

Jim: Please.

Katherine: You'll be here. I'll be in a grand ballroom with stars for chandeliers. *(Turning to him)* Shush. Stop. It'll be easier for you. You'll be free of all this too, you'll be able to dance away free. That's what I wanted to say. What I wanted you to know. That I knew all the time and that there'll be no need to feel guilty. Just be free, fly away. No more me wetting the bed, no more nights of me lying there keeping you awake, asking you to play games and pretend. I want you to forgive me too, for the hardship, and for leaving you. If I went on any longer it'd be tubes and pipes and oxygen masks and God knows what. You wouldn't be able to mind me.

Jim: I would, I will.

Katherine: Jim, Jim.

Jim: Just a fall. We just fell over. It's not the end of the world/

Katherine: No.

Jim: You'll be all right.

Katherine: Fixed like magic.

Jim: I'll take better care of you. I'll/

Katherine: Be free of me.

Jim: No … No. I won't. I can't.

Katherine: You will. Please. You have to.

Jim: Why? We can take care of you. I'll ask Nora to come home. She can take time off, Ger would come home. She would if you asked her. She's a nurse. Kate we can/

Katherine: No. You're not listening again. The children are in their own lives.

Nora, **Ger** *and* **Francie** *have begun to appear from their three separate points on the stage. They are converging on the place where their parents are lying. They seem to look at them but not at each other.*

Nora: I can't get down this evening. I'm too knackered Paddy. Nobody knows what those kids take out of me. And I hate driving in the dark and the rain. I'll go down tomorrow. Maybe you'll come with me.

Ger: When I'm not in love I can't seem to see anything as worthwhile. Everything seems so dull and plain. So ordinary. Just eating and working and sleeping. It kills me. What are we, just organs? Just kidneys and livers and blood. Then I meet someone and it's like … it's like a curtain opening and lights going up. Like a different world, a fantasy, romance. And we're dreams and loving and wonderful. It's suddenly wonderful. Like we're playing around the garden, around the tree before dinner. Chops and onions on Saturdays. Those were the happy days there. *(Pause)* I don't want to go home now. I don't want to be failed kidneys and diseased livers. Trips to the bathroom through that house. I couldn't bear it. Not there. That's not

the Mother I have with me here. Here I have the one that
sees the things I see, the one that knows why I have to be in
love, the one that understands that and wants it too for me,
that sees my father in me too and knows it's all part of a
long exhausting exhilarating dance. *(Pause)* That she is part
of too.

Nora: He's taking care of her. He never left her, no matter.
That's what I think when I go down and see them. He is
there with her. He wasn't the one ran away. Not really. And
wasn't that something? Wasn't that true loving too?

Francis: And Bohm concluded that the particle in Area B
somehow knew at the moment it happened that the state of
its space-like separated partner in Area A had also changed.
This leads us to the possibility that there may be a faster-
than-light communication of a type conventional physics
cannot explain. Looked at this way, what happens in one
place is intimately and immediately connected to what
happens elsewhere. All the parts are seen to be in immediate
connection, what is called the notion of 'the unbroken
wholeness'.

Life is not static, it is kinetic. Human DNA vibrates at
52 to 78 gigahertz. We broadcast on our own frequencies
and pulse our particles into each other. Imagine. Imagine it
like particles communicating across the void. Imagine she
knows. All our thoughts, all the time. Imagine she is
connected into our lives all the time, wherever we go,
whatever we do. That it's never pulled out. Never cut off.
Imagine. Imagine she knows. She knows and has known all
along. She knows. *(Pause)* And she forgives him. And she
forgives him. And me. And Ger and Nora too. All of us.
And she's not there in that cold post office now in the
middle of the night where I dream she might have fallen
down and he with her. She's not there. She's not there.
She's not in pain; for we are there for her, some parts of us
always. And they are the real. This is the reality; where Ger
and Nora and I carry our parents about on our backs like

the wings of fabled spirits. *(Jim and Katherine rise onto the hands of Nora and Ger. They stand behind them)* For better or worse, imagine, their griefs and taints ours, their flaws and marvels all inescapably ours and part of us. Part of the same energy. No easier to cut free from or disconnect than our own arms and legs. Imagine. Like wings. That's the way it is. That's the real. That's the way it is tonight.

Francis puts on the Fred Astaire version of 'The Way You Look Tonight' and stands in his room in California while it plays. Ger and Nora sway separately. Katherine and Jim stand out on the floor.

Katherine: This one always makes me feel light as a feather. Shall we?

Jim: Certainly Mrs Dooley.

They dance, wonderfully.

Katherine: *(While dancing)* You dance so well.

Jim: You're passable yourself.

Katherine: Gracious, what grace!

Jim: Watch this! *(He twirls her)*

Katherine: Amazing what a little polish can do.

Jim: You're like air in my arms.

And she is. He is dancing without her without knowing it. Katherine spins through the spaces of Ger and Nora, with them and not quite with them, and then to Francis. She moves with him for a few steps. And then she is gone, back to Jim just as the music ends and the lights are coming down again. Katherine and Jim hold each other. The children are still there.

Katherine: *(Her head on his shoulder, whispers)* Caherconn, hello?

The children turn towards their parents.

Francis: Dad?

Nothing moves. A long beat.

Ger: Dad?

Nora: Dad? Mam?

Francis: Mam?

*And the lights fade slowly on **Katherine** and **Jim** leaving the three children like satellites. A moment. Then we go softly into dark.*

THE END